From Sea to Shining Sea

50 Daily Devotions from Traveling to
Every State in America

H. Eugene and Marsha Frame
with John Christopher Frame

Contents

Introduction

By John Christopher Frame

"There's blood all over!" my sister screamed. She was crying when my parents rushed into the bathroom to see what the problem was.

I was five years old and had slipped in the shower, scraping the back of my head. We were in Grand Cayman, an island in the Caribbean, staying there for six weeks while my dad served as an interim pastor. My parents bandaged my head and our life continued normally, with us enjoying experiences together in a place new to all of us.

Grand Cayman was where I learned to swim. My memories there also include drinking powdered milk, watching *Old Yeller* too many times, and running out on the porch when we heard airplanes flying over as they prepared to land. They flew so low it almost seemed like we could reach out and touch them.

My parents' willingness to take their young family to Grand Cayman was just one chapter of the larger adventure of their life together. Early in their marriage, they sold their newly built brick house and moved away when my dad felt called to study for the ministry. In their nearly sixty years of marriage, they've lived in four states and met a goal of visiting all fifty. Throughout this journey, they've sought to keep God at the center of their marriage.

My parents are retired now and live a few miles away from their hometown and that brick house they sold years ago. They still plan affordable vacations. But they enjoy having a picnic in a nearby park just as much as going on a trip.

My parents aren't big spenders, and they don't plan luxurious vacations. They don't ski, golf, or lie on the beach. When they travel, they visit historical places, national parks, and state capitol buildings. My mom was a teacher and loves nature and American history. I'm not sure my dad has always been interested in all the places my mom has enjoyed visiting, but they always go together. And half the fun is planning the trip. They do that together too.

This book is a project my parents and I completed together. It's a way for us to share about their travels around the United States. More importantly, it's a way to help you on your spiritual journey.

There is one short devotion for each of the fifty states. Each one has a main idea to reflect on, and at the end of it is a question or two to think about, a Bible verse, and one or two prayer points. Throughout, my parents share snapshots of a lifetime of journeys—from riding cross-country on a bus to a youth convention in California, to visiting the "Field of Dreams" in Iowa, to panning for gold in a shallow creek in South Dakota.

Maybe you picked up this book because you love traveling, or you enjoy traveling vicariously through the stories of others. Maybe you're curious to read what is written about a particular state. Or you're looking for a daily devotional to help reignite your spiritual routine and nourish your soul. Over the next fifty days, you'll learn about places in the United States you never knew existed and recall some of the places you love. In some ways, it will be like you're taking a journey with us. Most importantly, you'll be quietly challenged to reflect and grow closer to God.

May the experiences and spiritual reflections captured in this book inspire you in your own journey of life and support you in your walk with God.

Let's go and explore!

1

Alabama

DREAMS

In the middle of Montgomery, Alabama, is a tall red-brick church with a white steeple. From the outside, the front of the building is perfectly symmetrical, with two sets of white stairs leading up to the main entrance and a narrow window on each side of the front door.

This is the Dexter Avenue King Memorial Baptist Church, and we had walked here from the Alabama State Capitol building, about five minutes away. Our son John was with us, and we had stopped on our way to Florida to visit our daughter and spend Christmas together as a family.

This Baptist church is now designated as a National Historic Landmark, and Marsha took a picture of John standing next to the sign. It said the church was built in 1885, that the Reverend Martin Luther King Jr. served as the pastor from 1954 to 1960, and that the Montgomery Bus Boycott was organized here.

We remember the days of the 1960s. Martin Luther King Jr. had a dream that our nation could be changed. His dream was that, regardless of who we are or what we look like, we would all live together in peace. Isn't this what God desires too?

How beautiful it would be if everyone lived out God's love and there was total peace in the world. No wars. No jealousy or anger toward others. No family conflicts.

How different things would be if everyone had a dream and desire to value and love others, and if this could become reality. Wars would end. Gangs would put down their guns. People who are divided would live together in unity.

May we all seek God and live in harmony. May we have dreams of developing greater love for others, and may we live that out each day.

Reflect

What is my dream for the world to be a better place?

Read

Matthew 22:37–39: *Jesus answered, "'Love the Lord your God with all your heart, soul and mind.' This is the first and most important command. And the second command is like the first: 'Love your neighbor as you love yourself.'"*

Pray

That I will seek harmony with others.

That I will live out God's love each day.

2

Alaska

CHANGE

One of the pictures we took in Alaska was from the back of a ferry. The ferry left behind a white trail on the surface of the deep, dark water, and there were mountains in the far distance. Heavy clouds hung overhead. Though the picture looks a little haunting, it's a snapshot of something Alaska is well known for—its nature and beauty.

Another photo we took was of the Alaska state bird, called the Willow Ptarmigan (pronounced with a silent "P"). It has feathered feet and is a member of the grouse family. That picture turned out blurred, as we were too far away from the bird and thought it might quickly fly away. But we bought a postcard with a picture of the bird on it, and like the postcard, the one we saw was brownish, blending into the grass along the road.

This bird goes through remarkable changes every year. It changes color from light brown in summer to snow white in winter to stay protected from predators. This is part of its life. Maybe it doesn't even realize it's changing.

As humans, change is something we also experience, in one way or another. Depending on what it is, we might fuss or grumble. Or we may appreciate the change if we think it's helpful.

Like the Alaska state bird that camouflages itself, transforming from brown to white, change is often good for us. Yet, we may struggle with it at first—like changing from old ways to new ways to become more like Christ.

With the Spirit of God living in us, we can experience supernatural support to change, transforming and becoming different than we once were.

Reflect

What changes in my life would make my relationship with God stronger?

Read

Philippians 1:6: *God began doing a good work in you. And he will continue it until it is finished when Jesus Christ comes again.*

Pray

For help to make any changes I think God wants me to make.

3

Arizona

FAMILY

We don't often get the chance to spend time together as a family. We live in Ohio, our daughter Tricia lives in Florida, and our son John lives overseas. But in 2019, we had an opportunity to vacation together in Arizona.

As a family, we visited a lavender farm, attended a Hillsong Church service, and saw ancient wood that had become stone at Petrified Forest National Park. We also visited the Chapel of the Holy Cross—built into a sandstone mountain, with reddish orange mountains as its natural backdrop. When you look up at the chapel from the road below, it looks like it's bursting out from the mountain. From there, you see a huge cross in the middle of the chapel's front wall of glass.

At the entrance, a sign near the door states "Peace to all who enter." Inside is a life-sized bronze statue of Jesus crucified on the Tree of Life. There are simple wooden benches to sit on and small candles in red glasses that visitors can light.

When we'd been to Arizona years before with our church's youth group, we'd only been able to spend a few minutes at this chapel. But on this trip, we were able to appreciate it more. And this time, we were here with our children.

Family members can be spread in many directions, especially when the kids get older and are out on their own. This trip allowed us to reconnect as a family, and we were thankful for that opportunity.

Spending time with those we love can require being intentional. As we think about our family, may we remember the good experiences we've had together. If we're fortunate to still have family members with us here on earth, let's ask God how he can use us to connect with and show love to our family.

Reflect

What can I do to make more time with the ones I love, and those who love me?

Read

Mark 3:23-25: *So Jesus called the people together and used stories to teach them. He said, "Satan will not force his own demons out of people. A kingdom that fights against itself cannot continue. And a family that is divided cannot continue."*

Pray

To be thankful for family.

For those who feel alone and are without a family.

4

Arkansas

REFRESH

We love going to parks. So, when we were in Arkansas, we visited Hot Springs National Park.

The visitor center is in a historical building made of brick and stone, with stained-glass ceilings. It's all been restored to its former grandeur. The museum has displays about the hot springs and the history of the town of Hot Springs, Arkansas, which gave us a sense of how popular this area was in the early 1900s.

Relaxing in rocking chairs on the front porch of the visitor center, we looked at a map and pamphlets and decided where to go next in the park. Around the area, hot water from underground is pumped up into fountains or is available by turning on a faucet. It's easy to touch the water or fill up bottles to take home. We met a woman who was filling gallon jugs with hot water; she was friendly and showed us how the faucets worked.

Nearby, Marsha touched hot water from a fountain. The water spewed up about twelve inches high from what looked like a candelabra. It flows continuously, and children came to put their hands in it, splashing each other and squealing.

That day, we walked along the half-mile Grande Promenade—a wide brick walkway with park benches—and then followed a nature trail to a hot spring that flowed into a shallow pool with rocks around it. Marsha sat down and slowly put one foot at a time into the soothing hot water. She has suffered from rheumatoid arthritis since she was sixteen years old, so she does everything carefully. We rested and were refreshed that day. Our strength was renewed.

As we go about our daily lives, we can get tired. Having intentional times when we can be refreshed in some way can help us on our journey of life.

May we feel the Lord refreshing us. And just like these hot springs, may we also be refreshing to others.

Reflect

> How am I taking time to be refreshed in my daily life?

Read

> Isaiah 58:11: *The Lord will always lead you.*
> *He will satisfy your needs in dry lands.*
> *He will give strength to your bones.*
> *You will be like a garden that has much water.*
> *You will be like a spring that never runs dry.*

Pray

> That the Lord will refresh my spirit.
> To be refreshing to others.

5

California

FRIENDSHIP

We both grew up in the same church in Ohio. In the summer of 1966, our youth group went on a twelve-day trip to attend an international youth convention in California. The trip cost us $100 each, and the rest of the expenses came from working together selling donuts and candy before we went.

Youth and chaperones from three other churches joined us. We didn't know each other at first, so this was an opportunity to make new friends. We all traveled on two buses across the country, from Ohio all the way to San Diego, California, and back. Each day, our youth pastor gave us an envelope with cash in it for our food.

We stopped along the way to eat, stretch, and sight-see—visiting places like the Gateway Arch in St. Louis and the Grand Canyon, and, when we could, eating at a Roy Rogers Restaurant. (In our Texas devotion later in this book, we share more memories from this trip.)

We were all excited when we finally crossed the California state line. In San Diego, some of us posed for a picture in front of the convention hall's sign that said "Welcome Church of God Convention."

Throughout the convention, there was a spirit of unity in the worship services and conferences. We all laughed together at a performance of a Charlie Brown play. And one evening we all enjoyed a harbor cruise in San Diego and saw naval warships in the bay.

In California, we visited several attractions, like Disneyland and SeaWorld, and saw the handprints and footprints of Joan Crawford, Sophia Loren, and other movie stars at the Grauman's Chinese Theater in Hollywood. And of course we went to the beach.

We loved every minute in California. This trip was an opportunity to deepen friendships with those in the group we knew, while building new friendships with those we'd just met.

When we returned to Ohio, a large group was gathered outside the church waiting for us. Our families were waving, and some were crying with relief to welcome us home. We'd had the cross-country trip of a lifetime, making memories with old and new friends.

May we ask God to help us build friendships with the right people—friendships that allow us to build each other up and that help us in our walk with God.

Reflect

What small thing can I do this week to build better relationships with old and new friends?

Read

Ephesians 4:2-3: *Always be humble and gentle. Be patient and accept each other with love. You are joined together with peace through the Spirit. Do all you can to continue together in this way. Let peace hold you together.*

Pray

To be the friend someone needs.

6

Colorado

CHOICES

The Four Corners Monument is where the four states of Colorado, Arizona, Utah, and New Mexico all come together. Their corners meet here, and it's the only point where four states in the United States come together.

The names of the four states are written in large letters at the site, and each state's flag flies high in the air. Nearby, Native Americans had artwork, scarves, and jewelry beautifully displayed in booths, and Marsha bought magnets and souvenirs.

Where the actual four corners of these states meet, there is a small brass plate. It's embedded in a pink granite circle that has these words carved into the outer edge: "Four states here meet in freedom under God." Visitors line up to take photos at this spot. Some people lie down and put an arm and a leg in each state so they're in all four states at the same time. We took a picture of Gene's feet—his left foot in New Mexico, his right foot in Colorado.

Standing at this spot where these four states meet, it's easy to choose which state you'd like to step into. It's laid out clearly. You could stand in Utah and then take one step and you'd be in Colorado. But making choices in life isn't always easy. In fact, life is complicated most of the time. Each day we're faced with choices that can determine what happens that day and beyond.

In the choices we make each day, may we choose to serve and live for God. And may God help us make decisions and choose the right way.

Reflect

How do I seek God when making decisions?

Read

Joshua 24:15b: *"You must choose for yourselves today. You must decide whom you will serve."*

Pray

For wisdom in making decisions.

For the Holy Spirit to guide me as I consider choices in life.

Want to see snapshots from these journeys?

Watch a 3-minute photo collage video featuring some highlights from Gene and Marsha's travels. Just add your name and email here:

https://johnchristopherframe.com/photo-collage

7

Connecticut

VALUING CHILDREN

The Connecticut State Capitol building has a dome covered with gold leaf, making it look something like a king's crown. The building was built in a Victorian Gothic design with New England granite and marble.

When we entered the building, we were asked if we'd like to join a group of third graders to hear a talk by a state representative. We said yes to this unique opportunity, which took place in the biggest room in the building—the House of Representatives Chamber, with stained-glass windows and dark wooden panels on the walls.

The children seemed interested in what the state representative was saying. She talked about how laws are made and asked whether any of them saw problems in their school or neighborhood that they'd like to see improved. A few students spoke up, and she affirmed all their concerns were important.

The state representative also showed them a Connecticut state quarter and asked how many had one. Several of the children raised their hands. They all seemed to know that a large oak tree, called the Charter Oak, was engraved on the back of the quarter. Then she told everyone to look down at the blue carpet. The children recognized the light-yellow designs in the carpet of the state seal, and they talked about the meaning of the seal.

We were impressed with this representative's demeanor and how well she kept the children's attention. She showed the importance of valuing children and teaching them well.

It might be easy to overlook those in society, like children, who we may not feel are making a large contribution. We may be busy with our own lives and not think about giving time and attention to others. But children, just like everyone else, deserve to feel valued.

Their curious minds need attention and guidance, and their souls need our gentle care.

Reflect

Am I a good example to the children around me? How could I improve in valuing others, including children?

Read

Matthew 19:14: *But Jesus said, "Let the little children come to me. Don't stop them, because the kingdom of heaven belongs to people who are like these children."*

Pray

For children who do not feel valued.

8

Delaware

FREEDOM

In the middle of the city of Dover, Delaware, is a grassy, rectangular-shaped park with tall trees. It's called The Green, and in the 1700s, it was used as a place to gather troops during the American Revolutionary War. One of the original buildings around The Green was the Golden Fleece Tavern. A red-brick building now stands where this tavern once was.

The Golden Fleece Tavern has a special historical significance. On December 7, 1787, the U.S. Constitution was approved there by the thirty appointed delegates from Delaware. The Constitution had been sent to all the states for approval, and Delaware was the first state to approve it. Because of this, Delaware is still called the "First State."

About a five-minute walk away from this site is the Delaware State Capitol—a building that looks like it belongs on the campus of an Ivy League university. It's built with red bricks, has white frames around the windows, and has a tall white cupula on the roof.

In front of the capitol building is a bronze statue of three men: an army officer from Delaware, a French military officer who came to support American independence in the Revolutionary War, and an enslaved African American who also fought in this war.

This statue represents the collective, diverse fight for American freedom, and engraved in the statue's granite base is the phrase "Liberty and Independence."

Freedom is something we all need and desire. Yet, there is a different kind of freedom we all need too. The Bible says we're all slaves to sin—something we need freedom from. The Apostle Paul wrote, "What a miserable man I am! Who will free me from this life dominated by sin? Thank God, the answer is in Jesus Christ" (Romans 7:24 NLT).

Instead of being dominated by sin, as Paul wrote, we can experience freedom through Christ living in us.

Reflect

What sins do I need freedom from?

Read

John 8:36: *"So if the Son makes you free, then you will be truly free."*

Pray

To be free from sin.

9

Florida

SUPREMACY

Standing alongside other visitors at Kennedy Space Center, we were all silent as we listened to the "National Anthem" being played through speakers and watched the U.S. flag being hoisted up the flagpole. Thick clouds provided a gray backdrop for the flag, but the sun was trying to break through and shine. A young man in front of us gazed at the flag through binoculars.

It was Christmas morning 2017, and we were in Florida visiting our daughter. That day, we saw tall rockets, a moon rock, and the inside of the *Atlantis* space shuttle. There were displays about our nation's space projects, from Project Mercury all the way to the International Space Station, which took its first occupants in the year 2000.

Standing near the Vehicle Assembly Building—52 stories tall, 518 feet wide, and reported to be one of the largest buildings in the world—gave us an idea of the size of the rockets that launch up into space.

Growing up, we heard of the desire for humans to go to the moon. And we remember the day in 1969 when Neil Armstrong was the first person to walk on the moon. Scientists continue to gain knowledge of other planets, our solar system, and our galaxy, and they say there are many other galaxies beyond our own. Wikipedia says it's estimated that between 200 billion to 2 trillion galaxies exist in the observable universe.

So, we are not really able to comprehend the vastness of space. And because we are human, it's difficult to completely fathom the vastness of God who made it all.

The supremacy and awesomeness of God is something to ponder.

Reflect

How might reflecting on the vastness of the universe help me better understand the supremacy of God who created it?

Read

Isaiah 40:28: *Surely you know. Surely you have heard. The Lord is the God who lives forever. He created all the world. He does not become tired or need to rest. No one can understand how great his wisdom is.*

Pray

That God, who is the creator of the universe, will be more fully Lord of my life.

10

Georgia

HARDSHIPS

President Franklin Delano Roosevelt (FDR) had a house built in Warm Springs, Georgia, about seventy-five miles south of Atlanta. Warm water that naturally came from the ground there was therapeutic to his legs, which had become paralyzed when he was thirty-nine.

FDR's house is called the "Little White House," and it's where he passed away in 1945. The house is open to the public, along with a museum and a nearby swimming pool.

The Little White House is one story, with six rooms. It has four white pillars on the front, and a wood-burning stove chimney sticks out of the roof. On the inside is dark wood paneling, like a cabin in the forest might have. FDR's chair is still near the stone fireplace, and his bedroom, where he died, has a bed with a white bedspread.

A little over a mile from the house and museum is the swimming pool FDR used, fed by the area's warm springs. It's drained now and not in use. We walked down steps into the empty pool, where there's a small knee-high basin with warm water from the springs. We have a picture of Marsha touching the water.

In the museum next to the Little White House, we looked at the display of FDR's canes and took a picture of his 1938 Ford Convertible. We learned about FDR's life as we read the signs throughout the museum. One had this quote, from an undelivered address, "The only limit of our realization of tomorrow will be our doubts of today. Let us move forward with strong and active faith."

Gene had a special interest in visiting this place because he had polio as a child. This was the disease FDR was diagnosed with (though, more recently, some researchers believe he may have had a different disease, Guillain-Barré syndrome). Gene was nineteen months old when he contracted polio. There was no vaccine at that time, and the disease affected his left leg, making him suddenly unable to walk. He was quarantined in a hospital for about a week, where his parents visited him through a glass window.

At the age of four, Gene had his first corrective surgery. He wore a brace on his left leg and for years had to wear special shoes. But this hardship didn't slow him down, and he enjoyed playing baseball and basketball with his friends. To this day, though, he walks with a slight limp that most don't notice.

At the museum, Gene recognized displays about old treatments and therapies for polio. A lump came to his throat as he pondered the days when he had polio and how blessed he was to have survived it and to be able to walk.

Experiences we have, such as visiting a place, may lead us to reflect on the past. We can recall how we've made it through tough times, and how we may have felt God's presence through it all.

May we all trust God to help us through our hardships, whatever they may be.

Reflect

How have I sensed God's presence when going through hardships?

Read

Romans 5:3-5a: *And we also have joy with our troubles because we know that these troubles produce patience. And patience produces character, and character produces hope. And this hope will never disappoint us, because God has poured out his love to fill our hearts.*

Pray

To grow closer to God during hardships.

Free Bonus Devotion

There's one more devotion from Georgia that couldn't fit into this book. It takes you to President Jimmy Carter's hometown and invites you to reflect on legacy—how you hope to be remembered. Here is the link to receive it free by email:

https://johnchristopherframe.kit.com/bonus -devotion

11

Hawaii

REMEMBRANCE

We went to Hawaii to celebrate our twenty-fifth wedding anniversary.

While we were there, Gene preached a sermon one Sunday morning at a Church of God church that is built on a mountaintop overlooking the Pacific Ocean. We also flew in a helicopter over volcanoes, seeing their smoke and lava, and we visited the "Painted Church," a Catholic church with columns that look like maroon candy canes. Bible stories are beautifully painted on the inside walls.

At the *USS Arizona* Memorial at Pearl Harbor, the atmosphere was solemn and sacred. This was where the surprise bombing against the United States took place in 1941. We first heard a presentation by National Park staff, then all of us visiting filed out in silence to board small boats that took us out to the actual memorial in the ocean. There, a white building is built over top of the sunken but still visible *USS Arizona* (a large warship). The names on the wall of the memorial (those killed in the bombing) seemed endless, and the "black tears"—drops of oil that rise to the surface from the ship below the water—were sobering.

The memorial at Pearl Harbor is a way to remember those who were killed, and it teaches future generations about what happened. A memorial reminds us of something. In this case, it was a horrible event.

Memorials can also serve the purpose of remembering something good. In the Bible, altars and memorials were built to honor God and remember what God had done. The Book of Joshua records a memorial being set up to remember the miraculous event of crossing the Jordan River on dry ground (Joshua 4). By marking the place where something happened that they wanted to remember, the people would be encouraged not to forget about it.

This kind of memorial was important for the Israelites, and it's important for us too. May we be reminded of the experiences that we want to remember because they were positive.

May we not forget God's presence with us along our journey.

Reflect

What can I do to better remember what God has done?

Read

Joshua 4:6-7: *"They will be a sign among you. In the future your children will ask you, 'What do these rocks mean?' Tell them the Lord stopped the water from flowing in the Jordan. When the Ark of the Covenant with the Lord crossed the river, the water was stopped. These rocks will help the Israelites remember this forever."*

Pray

To remember positive experiences and enjoy good memories.

12

Idaho

IMPRISONMENT

I n Idaho, we visited the Idaho Potato Museum, where there's a giant fiberglass sculpture of a baked potato, complete with butter and sour cream. We also visited the Oregon Trail, the state capitol building, and a former prison, the Old Idaho State Penitentiary.

It may seem surprising that a former prison is a popular tourist attraction, but it gets about thirty thousand visitors a year. This former prison is on the National Register of Historic Places. It has a beautiful garden, with red, pink, and white roses; yellow butter cups; and snow queen oakleaf hydrangeas. The garden and beige stone walls of the historical buildings give the place a European look. One of the main buildings even looks something like a castle, while other buildings resemble a monastery complex.

On the outside, everything is beautiful. But this place is no castle or monastery. The garden and stone buildings mask the harshness of what this place used to be. It was a prison for 101 years, from 1872 to 1973, when it was closed after prisoners rioted over the living conditions. Executions even took place there.

Stepping inside and hearing the steel doors clang behind us was frightening. The windows had iron bars, and some of the cells had metal lattice doors while others were traditional bars.

We took a picture of one cell that had light green walls, a dark-gray toilet, a sink with hot- and cold-water taps, and a small table. The metal-frame cot had a white sheet and thin pillow on top that resembled a padded door mat. In the early days, prisoners used a bucket for their toilet. It was not, nor was it intended to be, a welcoming place.

Since Adam and Eve, people have done wrong. Adam and Eve were told what the consequence was for their sin, and they were filled with shame and guilt. Still today, there are consequences for doing wrong. There is physical imprisonment for committing a crime. But there is also the imprisonment of a guilty conscience, whether our sin is technically illegal or not.

Thankfully, the Lord can release us from the imprisonment of a guilty conscience and of the sin that causes it. The Lord is ready to change the lives of those who earnestly seek him and desire freedom, asking for his forgiveness.

Reflect

Is there any sin that I need freedom from?

Read

Psalm 107:13-15: *In their misery they cried out to the Lord. And he saved them from their troubles. He brought them out of their gloom and darkness. He broke their chains. Let them give thanks to the Lord for his love and for the miracles he does for people.*

Pray

To be free from the imprisonment of sin.

For those who are imprisoned—behind literal bars or the bars of sin.

13

Illinois

SUPPORT

In January 2014, we drove to Chicago to visit the Pacific Garden Mission, an organization that serves people who are homeless, ministering to anyone who walks through their doors. Through their different ministries, the Pacific Garden Mission provides support to many, and they've been doing so since it was founded in 1877.

They also record a weekly radio program, heard on over 3,100 radio stations, called "Unshackled!" It's a half-hour old-time radio program, with each episode narrating the life of a person who was changed by Christ.

We drove to Chicago because the story of Marsha's grandfather, Jack Crowe, was going to be featured on "Unshackled!" We had submitted his story to them. He was a Kentucky farmer who turned from a poker player to an evangelist, and who was later tragically killed in a tornado while getting ready to preach a revival service.

We wanted to be present to hear his story recorded for the radio program. On the stage, each voice actor had a chair and microphone. In front of the stage was a Christmas tree with white lights. A sign above read "To God be the glory, great things He has done." The recording was later broadcast as episode #3302.

When we first arrived that day, and before we attended the recording, we were invited to tour the facility. We saw where the people they serve sleep. They have 750 beds for men and 250 for women and children. There are two libraries with computers and spaces for Bible studies, support group meetings, and educational classes. There's also a greenhouse and a landscaped courtyard. We were invited to eat a meal in their large dining hall and attend their 5:00 p.m. service.

We were impressed by all we experienced and learned that day. It was a welcoming atmosphere, with friendly faces and people speaking with each other. The Pacific Garden Mission provides ministry to many who are in need—from supporting those on the streets of Chicago, to those in their homes around the world listening to their radio program. They do this so others can know that, as a sign on the outside of their building says, "JESUS SAVES."

Their work and ministry can remind us that we all need support in some way or another. There's no shame in needing support. And while large organizations like this one provide assistance to many people at one time, we as individuals can also support others, encouraging and helping them in whatever ways we can.

Reflect

In what ways can I best support others?

Read

Galatians 6:2: *Help each other with your troubles. When you do this, you are obeying the law of Christ.*

Pray

To be wise, discerning, and generous in providing support to others.

You can listen to this episode of "Unshackled!" online:

"Unshackled!" website:
https://unshackled.org/program/jack-crowe

YouTube:
Search for *Unshackled Jack Crowe*.

14

Indiana

CHALLENGES

The Indiana Dunes State Park, on the southern shore of Lake Michigan, has a sand dune that is nearly two hundred feet tall. Sand dunes are huge mounds of sand that grow and shift from wind over time. Tall grasses partially cover the dunes, helping to reduce erosion and stabilize their shape.

During our visit to this state park, families were walking up the dunes. Children were playing, sometimes falling on the soft sand. Walking in sand can be challenging in general, and walking up a hill of sand is even more of a struggle as you try to keep your balance in the moving sand under your feet.

We can't remember whether we made it to the top of the large sand dune that day. The trip was too long ago, and we must not have had our camera with us, because we can't find any pictures from that trip. We probably did make it to the top, though, as we were younger then. We more easily pressed through challenges we faced, even if that meant going slowly.

For those who make it to the top of a dune at the park, the view is quite amazing. So, while the journey up can be difficult, the reward at the top is wonderful.

Like walking up a sand dune, our path in life is not always easy. Life has its ups and downs, its successes and failures. There are countless obstacles along the way, and we might even fall down a few times. The challenge is to keep moving forward despite the missteps or difficulties along the journey.

Regardless of the challenges we face in life, let's always aim for heaven as our goal. When we focus on heaven, along with God's presence with us today, we may feel differently about the challenges we currently face.

Keeping our eyes on Christ, we can face life's challenges with a heavenly perspective—and continue our journey, upward and onward.

Reflect

How can keeping a focus on heaven help me during my challenges?

Read

Philippians 3:13-14: *Brothers, I know that I have not yet reached that goal. But there is one thing I always do: I forget the things that are past. I try as hard as I can to reach the goal that is before me. I keep trying to reach the goal and get the prize. That prize is mine because God called me through Christ to the life above.*

Pray

For strength through challenges.

15

Iowa

RECONCILIATION

In the middle of hundreds of acres of cornfields in Iowa is the setting of the 1989 movie *Field of Dreams*. We were on our way back home from Yellowstone National Park (which we write about at the end of this book) when we stopped here for a visit. Our son John, who was twelve years old at the time, was with us.

The baseball field featured in the movie is open to visitors, and nearby is the two-story white farmhouse with a large wraparound porch and a white picket fence. It was a warm, sunny day, and the sky was blue and had large, fluffy white clouds.

John enjoyed sitting on the steel bleachers, walking the freshly mowed outfield, and running the bases on the field. He left with a *Field of Dreams* T-shirt, a dried ear of corn, a tube with some dirt in it, and a memorable experience he fondly recalls to this day.

You might be familiar with the storyline of the movie: The owner of the farm, walking among tall stalks of corn, heard a strange whisper: "If you build it, he will come." He began plowing up his cornfield to make a baseball field, and when he finished, his deceased father, as well as famous baseball players from the past, came to play on the field. At the end of the movie, the farmer and his dad meet and quietly reconcile, shaking hands and throwing a baseball back and forth on the field.

There's a story in the Bible that relates to dreams and reconciliation: the story of Joseph, in the Book of Genesis. It's fascinating. Joseph was a dreamer, and though his brothers wanted to kill him, they all reconciled years later.

In *Field of Dreams*, the farmer didn't know the meaning of his dream or that it would lead to him being reconciled with his dad. Through action that led to reconciliation, his life was changed for the better.

Reflect

What spiritual and emotional benefits come from reconciliation?

Read

Genesis 45:14-15: *Then Joseph hugged his brother Benjamin and cried. And Benjamin cried also. Then Joseph kissed all his brothers. He cried as he hugged them. After this, his brothers talked with him.*

Pray

For guidance if there is anyone I need to be reconciled with.

16

Kansas

PREJUDICE

O n a beautiful spring day, we visited the Kansas State Capitol building. It has a distinctive dome topped with dark copper that rises tall above the main part of the building.

We joined a tour led by a retired gentleman who wore a jacket and tie and was knowledgeable about all things Kansas. He talked about the official state song, "Home, Home on the Range," and we all sang it together:

> Oh, give me a home where the buffalo roam,

Where the deer and the antelope play;
Where seldom is heard a discouraging
word,
And the skies are not cloudy all day.

As we walked on the marble floors throughout the building, we stopped in front of painted murals that depict the history of the state. These included paintings of Native peoples, farms and animals, abolitionist John Brown, and President Dwight Eisenhower, who grew up in Kansas.

Eisenhower was president when the Supreme Court case *Brown v. Board of Education* was decided in 1954. In that case, the Supreme Court decided, "Separate educational facilities are inherently unequal," and racial segregation in public schools was ruled unconstitutional.

The Kansas State Capitol building is a little over a mile away from Monroe Elementary School, a two-story red-brick building that looks similar to the schools we'd attended as children. Years ago, this was a segregated school only for African American children. Today, it's a National Historic Site, commemorating the Supreme Court's decision on *Brown v. Board of Education*.

Inside is a museum, and there we saw a doll in a glass display case. It was one of four dolls used in the "doll test," an important psychological study with young African American children. In the study, children were asked questions about the dolls to see how they perceived them. Each doll was the same, except in its skin color. Most children preferred the white doll.

This study led to the conclusion that racial discrimination and segregation brought about inferior feelings in African American children. While this study took place years before the *Brown* v. *Board of Education* case, the findings played a role in the Supreme Court's decision.

This school and the segregation it represented are a reminder of prejudice in our world. We'd like to think that things are better now than they were in the past. Yet, a glance at the news tells us that not everyone feels equally valued and loved in our world. And while we may think of prejudice as something from the past, or existing only within other people, we can pray about any buried prejudices of our own.

May we think well of others, love everyone, and seek God's help for feelings within us that may need to change.

Reflect

In what ways might I struggle to feel love for all
people?

Read

Micah 6:8: *The Lord has told you what is good. He
has told you what he wants from you: Do what is
right to other people. Love being kind to others. And
live humbly, trusting your God.*

Pray

To remove any prejudice within me.

To be kind to all.

17

Kentucky

FEELINGS

Like many others who live in Ohio, our families came from Kentucky. We enjoy the mountains, people, and food of the state. We've driven through Kentucky countless times, and we experience different feelings in various parts of the state. For example . . .

We've loved going to the top of Natural Bridge—a huge rock formation that looks like a bridge—where we felt the beauty of nature when looking out at all the trees around it.

At Abraham Lincoln's birthplace, as well as when walking among the graves at Camp Nelson National Cemetery, we felt a sense of patriotism.

We felt wonder and refreshment when walking down the paved path into the depths of Mammoth Cave, feeling the cool, dry air from the cave. Even on a hot day, the cave stays around 54°F (12°C).

And though we don't gamble, we felt some excitement when taking a tour of the Churchill Downs racetrack and the Kentucky Derby Museum. It wasn't a race day, but we could imagine the thunderous sounds of horses pounding the dirt track and people cheering for their favorites.

We've had many memorable experiences in Kentucky. And with all those experiences come many different feelings.

In life, feelings come and go. We all love feeling happiness and joy, and we know the "warm fuzzies" we feel when thinking back on good times. Yet, feelings aren't always positive. Feelings that we don't want can have a powerful hold on us. Holding onto sadness, anger, or bitterness can affect us in negative ways, impacting our sleep or our relationships with others and God. Negative feelings can disrupt our hope and cloud our vision of what God wants for us.

So, here's a challenge for all of us: What if we focus more on what we believe rather than on how we feel? God knows us and how we feel. Through Christ, he has had similar experiences to us. God is with us, even when we feel low.

That is something to believe and remember, despite how we may feel.

Reflect

What are some of the best experiences I've had?

What feelings do I have when I remember those good times?

Read

Psalm 139:1-2: *Lord, you have examined me. You know all about me. You know when I sit down and when I get up. You know my thoughts before I think them.*

Pray

For the release of negative feelings that have a hold on my life.

18

Louisiana

ASSISTANCE

In Louisiana, we were eager to drive across a bridge that is the world's longest continuous span over water. The bridge is called Lake Pontchartrain Causeway, and it seemed endless, stretching nearly twenty-four miles long.

This bridge took us to New Orleans. It was a beautiful autumn day with a bright blue sky and no clouds, and we were starting a full day of sightseeing. Being history buffs, we drove to the Battle of New Orleans National Historic Park. We had grown up singing the song "The Battle of New Orleans" by Johnny Horton, and we learned about the American victory over the British there.

In downtown New Orleans, we went to Jackson Square and saw the majestic St. Louis Cathedral—a large church that looks European with three tall spires. At a nearby park, we admired boats on the Mississippi River. The surface of the river sparkled white from the bright sun.

We bought tickets for a bus tour of the city to do some sightseeing. One of the stops on the bus tour was at the City Park of New Orleans. Our friends had recommended we eat a local treat called beignets (soft, puffy fried pastries covered with powdered sugar), so we bought some in this park, at the Café Du Monde, and relaxed at a picnic table shaded by old oak trees with Spanish moss hanging down from their branches.

After the bus tour, we drove around the area on our own. We saw houses and buildings damaged by Hurricane Katrina in 2005 and wondered how long it would take for this bustling city to make a complete comeback.

There was so much to experience and see in New Orleans. Some of it we did on our own. But we did some things with the assistance of others—like the bus tour that took us around the city to assist us in our sightseeing.

And we probably wouldn't have tried those soft, sugary pastries if our friends hadn't told us about them.

In life, there are some things we can see and do on our own. With other things, though, we may benefit from others' assistance. In some cases, it may be impossible for us to do something without help. By accepting assistance, or reaching out for it, our lives can be improved.

Reflect

What could be better in my life if I reached out more for assistance?

Read

Ecclesiastes 4:9-10a: *Two people are better than one.*
They get more done by working together.
If one person falls, the other can help him up.

Pray

> To be able to assist those who need support.
>
> For courage to reach out for assistance when I need it.

19

Maine

PRAISE

Early in our marriage, we made a goal to travel to as many states as possible to visit national parks, historical sites, and landmarks. People we knew encouraged us to visit Acadia National Park in Maine. They'd say, "You've got to see Acadia." So, in 1993, we went and loved every minute of being at this remarkable park.

On one hike, we walked up a rugged trail to Bubble Rock—a giant gray boulder that looks like it's balancing on the edge of a mountain. We took John's picture while he touched it. On other excursions in the park, we marveled at the stunning views around

Jordan Pond, heard waves crashing at Thunder Hole, and looked up at Bass Harbor Head Lighthouse—a small lighthouse attached to a white house, all on a cliff above the Atlantic Ocean.

Our favorite place at Acadia was probably Cadillac Mountain—the most popular destination in the park. It's 1,530 feet high, and in the winter, it's the first place in the country to see the sunrise.

This area is the homeland of the Wabanaki, known as People of the Dawn, and we learned that people have enjoyed spectacular views from Cadillac Mountain for thousands of years. Sunrise and sunset are the most popular times to visit the mountain, and we went to see the sunset. A large crowd of people had gathered. Some stood, but many sat on boulders. We waited along with them, camera in hand, for the sun to set. There were dark-gray clouds that evening, yet the sunset created beautiful rays of yellow and orange that shined out.

Sunsets can remind us of God's creation, power, and presence. Not only are they beautiful times of the day, but they symbolize a beginning and an ending—newness and closure.

Sunrises and sunsets can be reminders to give God praise. Yet, we can praise God regardless of the time of day—before, during, or after sunrise or sunset. As the psalmist wrote, "From the rising of the sun unto the going down of the same the Lord's name is to be praised" (Psalm 113:3 KJV).

Reflect

When was the most recent sunrise or sunset I enjoyed watching?

Read

Psalm 113:2-4: *The Lord's name should be praised now and forever. The Lord's name should be praised from where the sun rises to where it sets. The Lord is supreme over all the nations. His glory reaches to the skies.*

Pray

To renew my desire to praise God.

20

Maryland

WANDERING

When our children were young and we lived in Arlington, Virginia, we drove to Maryland and visited Assateague Island one day. It's a narrow island, thirty-seven miles long and about one mile wide. The northern part of the island is in Maryland while the southern part is in Virginia.

We hiked two trails on the island, had a picnic, and went to the beach. We looked out at the Atlantic Ocean and felt the warm, soft sand on our feet. It brought smiles to our faces to see our two children having so much fun. Marsha had learned about this island and the wild horses that roam around it in a book called *Misty of Chincoteague* when she'd taken a children's literature class.

At the visitor center, we saw a film about wild horses on the island. Since it's been around forty years since then, it's hard to remember if we saw any horses that day. We probably did—from a far distance. Park rangers often told visitors where to look to be able to see them.

It's interesting that horses roam around this island. Wild and free, they can be anywhere, like on the beaches and in the campgrounds. They have the freedom to wander around. We humans can wander too, and in different ways, including wandering into sin.

So, let's stay close to God, allowing him to lead and guide us through life, so we can be free from the dangers of sin, and better resist drifting where temptations might take us.

Reflect

How willing am I to allow God to lead me?

Read

James 4:7-8: *So give yourselves to God. Stand against the devil, and the devil will run away from you. Come near to God, and God will come near to you. You are sinners. So clean sin out of your lives. You are trying to follow God and the world at the same time. Make your thinking pure.*

Pray

To not wander away from living in a way that pleases God.

21

Massachusetts

NOSTALGIA

For many, the name Norman Rockwell (1894–1978) brings back nostalgic memories of American family life and values.

We had followed the life of Norman Rockwell for many years, and when we lived in Michigan, we had a Rockwell print hanging on our living room wall. Called "Marriage License," this print shows a young couple in an office registering for their marriage license—the man tall and in a suit, and the woman in a yellow dress and high heels, standing on tiptoe at the tall wooden counter.

As a child, Marsha's dad had subscriptions to *The Saturday Evening Post* and *Boys' Life* magazine. Rockwell's paintings were often on the cover of these magazines, and everybody loved them. They were detailed and folksy, and communicated the values of the time.

In 1993, on our trip to Acadia National Park in Maine, we stopped in Stockbridge, Massachusetts, and visited the town where Rockwell had lived. The town is nearly three hundred years old and has only about two thousand residents.

This town was featured in Rockwell's famous painting "Home for Christmas," which almost makes you feel like you're walking in a small town in America. In the painting, you see snow-covered cars parked on Main Street. The buildings in the town are lit with a yellow glow, and a Christmas tree is visible in an upstairs window. Children are playing on the snowy street, and the sidewalk is full of people outside enjoying Christmastime. The painting gives you all the warm feelings of Christmas. Like many of Rockwell's paintings, "Home for Christmas" evokes a longing to go back to the way life used to be.

Before visiting the museum that holds the largest collection of Rockwell's drawings and paintings, we walked around downtown Stockbridge on the same

Main Street we'd seen in that painting. We went inside the general store, a gift shop, and the church. The beauty of this town was touching. The ambiance gave us a warm feeling, reminding us of our childhood years and the way times once were.

While we can't go back to the past (and many of us wouldn't want to even if we could), we can appreciate the experiences we've had and the nostalgic feelings they bring. We can remember good memories from the past, appreciating how those experiences have helped shape who we are today.

Reflect

What positive memory from the past can I think about today?

Read

Psalm 143:5-6: *I remember what happened long ago. I recall everything you have done. I think about all you have made. I lift my hands to you in prayer. As a dry land needs rain, I thirst for you.*

Pray

To be satisfied with simple things.

For uncomfortable memories to be replaced with positive ones.

22

Michigan

JOURNEYING

We lived in Michigan for twenty-one years while Gene pastored a church there.

Geographically, Michigan is made up of two parts: the Lower Peninsula and the Upper Peninsula. Connecting the two is the five-mile-long Mackinac Bridge. Every year on Labor Day, tens of thousands of people walk across this bridge, from north to south. For several years we wanted to do this, and we finally did on Labor Day in 1998. It was the 41st Annual Mackinac Bridge Walk.

Everyone walked swiftly on the left side of the bridge, while vehicles drove on the right. We were all on this journey together. The skies were cloudy, though it didn't rain. The walkers chattered softly. In front of us was a man wearing a red jacket with seven large cloth patches sewn on the back, each from a different year he had walked the bridge. It was a little scary to look down as we walked over the metal-grated section of the bridge. You can see, beneath your feet, deep water that connects two of Michigan's Great Lakes.

The walk lasted about ninety minutes, and we all received a certificate of completion at the finish line. We bought a patch that said "I walked the Mackinac Bridge in 1998." Gene remembers that by the end of the walk, he had to go to the bathroom badly. A long row of portable toilets sat at the finish line, but each one had a line of people waiting. Gene suffered while waiting but was able to make it to a different restroom a little farther away.

Overall, the walk was tiring, especially for Marsha, who has suffered from rheumatoid arthritis most of her life. We were glad we did it, though, and enjoyed being around everyone experiencing this journey together.

As Christians, we are all on a journey moving in the same direction—heavenward. But unlike the Mackinac Bridge, our life's journey is never a straight line. We might get off track and need to be redirected. Thankfully, we can find strength in experiencing our journey of life together with others.

May we ask God for wisdom and guidance as we press on in our journey.

Reflect

Where am I struggling in my journey?

What is going well?

Read

Proverbs 3:5-6: *Trust the Lord with all your heart. Don't depend on your own understanding. Remember the Lord in everything you do. And he will give you success.*

Pray

For God's guidance, peace, and protection on my journey of life.

23

Minnesota

Outcomes

The Mall of America is in Bloomington, Minnesota, a suburb of Minneapolis. It has over five hundred stores, around fifty restaurants, and a thirteen-screen movie theater, so you can shop till you drop! According to their website, the mall has more than thirty thousand indoor plants, including hundreds of trees. Several of our friends had been to this mall, and we thought we'd visit it too.

We arrived early, when it wasn't crowded, and walked around. We also went to the amusement park inside the mall that had a Ferris wheel, a carousel, and a log chute water ride. We sat on a bench to rest and take in all the excitement around us. Some people were gathering for a birthday party. Others were standing in line to ride the bumper cars. Parents were waving to their children as they enjoyed the rides. Everyone seemed happy.

The mall brings enjoyment to many. But this mall didn't always exist. Drastic changes were made to the land to build it. For example, part of the land had an old sports stadium on it. Another part was a natural area. Before this mall existed, there were birds flying and squirrels scampering around some of the land. Maybe deer were running through the area. So it's much different now than it used to be.

Sometimes the outcomes from change are positive. Other times, not so much. Sometimes it's a little of both. It's that way in our own lives as well. We make a change, big or small, and don't know what the outcome will be. We may not be sure whether we made the right decision. We may wonder whether we made the wrong one.

It's important to be mindful of how the decisions we make lead to outcomes. And in terms of choices and outcomes related to God's creation, let us be considerate of our environment, how we interact with it and change it, as nature is an essential part of our world.

May we seek God's wisdom and Spirit as we go through life, making decisions that, in some way or another, affect our lives. May we ask God to actively involve and intervene in our decisions and the outcomes that come from them.

Reflect

Do I pause to think about what positive or negative outcomes may result from decisions I make?

Read

Proverbs 14:15b: *But a wise person thinks about what he does.*

Pray

To seek the Lord's wisdom.

That God will be actively involved in my decisions and the outcomes that come from them.

24

Mississippi

SORROW

During the American Civil War, battles took place at what is now known as the Vicksburg National Military Park. Many soldiers died, as was always the case. We drove around the site, stopping to view grave sites and read inscriptions on monuments.

The battlefield is quiet now. We saw cannons, but there was no gunfire. No orders being shouted. Just an eerie, empty sense of courage and loss.

Going to places like this always gives us pause. We think about the families of the soldiers who'd worried about their loved ones in war—the constant fear they must have experienced, as well as their heartbreak when they learned their loved ones were wounded or killed. We pondered the devastation and loss of lives that had taken place on this site 150 years before. It's hard to imagine what emotions were felt by those on the battlefield.

War causes great sorrow. Thankfully, many of us are not directly affected by war. We don't feel the threat of bombs, nor do we have loved ones on the front line. But all of us, at some point or another, experience other kinds of sorrow, pain, and loss.

In these times, may we find support in the sorrow we're going through. May we remember the Holy Spirit's ability to bring us peace. May we remember to have hope in God who is our help.

As it's written in Psalms, "The Lord is close to the brokenhearted. He saves those whose spirits have been crushed" (Psalm 34:18).

Reflect

How can I pray for others and the sorrow they are experiencing?

Read

> Psalm 34:17-18: *The Lord hears good people when they cry out to him. He saves them from all their troubles. The Lord is close to the brokenhearted. He saves those whose spirits have been crushed.*

Pray

> For those in war today, and for their families.
>
> For people experiencing sorrow.

25

Missouri

SEEKING

One of the most famous landmarks in the United States is in St. Louis, Missouri—the Gateway Arch. At 630 feet tall, it's the tallest man-made monument in the country—taller than the Statue of Liberty and the Washington Monument.

We visited St. Louis as a family in 1986, a few years before our daughter Tricia went away to college, and went to the Gateway Arch. We have a photo of the sun reflecting brightly off the arch, which is stainless steel.

To get to the top of the arch, the four of us got into a small tram car. It was a tight squeeze for all of us, and the temperature was warm. We knew we were safe, but the trip up the arch still made us feel a bit uneasy.

At the top, we had views of the city of St. Louis and the Mississippi River, which is next to the arch. We took a picture of the shadow of the arch on the calm, brown river below (the river is wide enough that the entire shadow of the arch lay on top of it).

Opened in 1965, the Gateway Arch is referred to as the "Gateway to the West." It was built to commemorate the people years ago who had traveled west into undeveloped territory, as well as Thomas Jefferson's role in that with the Louisiana Purchase. Many people went west, traveling to find land to farm or planning to search for gold. They were all seeking something—prosperity, opportunity, or just a better way to survive.

Today, we're also likely seeking something in life. Maybe it's something we need or desire. Maybe it's relief from physical or emotional pain. Maybe we seek more hope to fill our hearts.

Years ago, families in America went west seeking something new. Today, we can follow Christ as we search for whatever it is we are seeking on our own journey of life.

Reflect

Am I seeking what pleases God?

Read

Matthew 7:7-8: *"Continue to ask, and God will give to you. Continue to search, and you will find. Continue to knock, and the door will open for you. Yes, everyone who continues asking will receive. He who continues searching will find. And he who continues knocking will have the door opened for him."*

Pray

That I seek what is good for me and others.

26

Montana

SPIRITUAL JOURNEY

We've made two trips to Glacier National Park in Montana. Both times, we crossed most of the country by Amtrak train and then rented a car. We enjoyed learning about the park, its geology, and Native peoples, and driving around to get a closer look.

The main road through Glacier National Park is called "Going-to-the-Sun Road." It's fifty miles long and crosses the Rocky Mountains, and has some of the most scenic views in the United States. There are blue-green lakes, dense forests, and, of course, large mountains. It's astonishing. One picture we took was of tall gray mountains reflected in a small lake. Another was of a stone mountain high above a dark-green evergreen forest.

Many people have traveled on this Going-to-the-Sun Road. And, to play on words, we know about the "Going-to-the-*Son* Road"—our spiritual journey with God, where we believe in the risen Christ, look to eternal life, and allow the Holy Spirit to live within us.

There are similarities with and differences between these two roads. The Going-to-the-Sun Road is closed for much of the year because of snow. Also, you need to pay an entry fee to enter Glacier National Park, where this road is. The Going-to-the-*Son* Road is always open, and because of Jesus's death on the cross, the penalty for our sin has already been paid.

Driving the Going-to-the-Sun Road takes about two hours, one way. There are many curves in the road, and drivers must be cautious because wild animals can suddenly appear on the road. The Going-to-the-*Son* Road is a lifetime spiritual journey. Caution is also needed, as evil is near. Things can discourage us and temptations can take us off track from our intended destination.

On the Going-to-the-Sun Road, there are no gas stations. But on the Going-to-the-*Son* Road, we can be refreshed and refueled through experiences with God that create glorious feelings that words cannot describe. You can travel both directions on the Going-to-the-Sun Road, and the view is just as impressive either way. But on the Going-to-the-*Son* Road, we always want to be going toward Christ, not away from him.

On our spiritual journey, may we always seek Christ who leads us in this life and into the life to come.

Reflect

How is my spiritual journey going?

Read

Matthew 7:13-14: *"Enter through the narrow gate. The road that leads to hell is a very easy road. And the gate to hell is very wide. Many people enter through that gate. But the gate that opens the way to true life is very small. And the road to true life is very hard. Only a few people find that road."*

Pray

> To always seek Christ and make daily decisions that support me in my spiritual journey.
>
> To stay focused on my eternal destination.

27

Nebraska

THE SOWER

The capitol building in Lincoln, Nebraska, looks much different than most other capitol buildings in the country. It's four hundred feet tall and was the first capitol in the United States built as an office tower.

In front of the building is a bronze statue of Abraham Lincoln wearing a long coat and holding his hands in front of him. "The Gettysburg Address" is carved into granite behind him.

On the very top of the building is a gold dome with another bronze statue atop it—a muscular man, about nineteen feet tall, sowing seeds with his right hand.

This statue is called "The Sower." High above the city, it symbolizes the agricultural heritage of Nebraska, where crops including soybeans and corn are grown.

The name of this statue reminds us of one of the parables of Jesus. In the Parable of the Sower, Jesus tells the story of a farmer planting seeds. These seeds fell on various places and had varying results. For example, seeds that fell on good soil grew and did well, some growing into plants that made one hundred times more grain (see Matthew 13:8).

When a farmer plants seeds, some will produce good results; some won't. The Parable of the Sower teaches us the importance of being "good soil": hearing and receiving the message of the Gospel, living accordingly, and growing—and helping others grow too—in the ways of Jesus.

Reflect

What mental images come to mind when I hear the Parable of the Sower?

Read

Matthew 13:3-8: *Then Jesus used stories to teach them many things. He said: "A farmer went out to plant his seed. While he was planting, some seed fell by the road. The birds came and ate all that seed. Some seed fell on rocky ground, where there wasn't enough dirt. That seed grew very fast, because the ground was not deep. But when the sun rose, the plants dried up because they did not have deep roots. Some other seed fell among thorny weeds. The weeds grew and choked the good plants. Some other seed fell on good ground where it grew and became grain. Some plants made 100 times more grain. Other plants made 60 times more grain, and some made 30 times more grain."*

Pray

To be the "good soil" that receives the message of the Gospel and lives accordingly.

28

Nevada

STORIES

The air was hazy from forest fires in California as we drove west across Nevada, and there was little change in scenery. Along the road, we saw Indian ricegrass, the Nevada state grass, swaying in the wind. We also saw sagebrush, the state flower. It has little yellow flowers and a pleasant smell, and seemed to be everywhere.

After driving five hundred miles that day, we arrived at our destination: Carson City, the capital of Nevada. This city is named after Kit Carson, who, among other things, was a rugged mountain man and animal trapper in the 1800s. The next morning, we went straight to the Nevada State Capitol building. On the grounds is a life-sized bronze statue of Kit Carson, leaning to his right and holding onto his hat while riding on a galloping horse.

Kit Carson is famous because of all the stories about his life. He played a part—not always a good one—in American history. Some of the things he did weren't good at all.

When we were children, he was a character in books and on TV. Stories were told of this cowboy-type man who traded furs. He had been a guide for western explorers, an army officer and, later in life, a federal Indian agent working for the U.S. government. So, he was a real person, even if all the stories about him may not have been.

Stories keep memories alive. And remembering positive stories from our own lives can help us think well about the past. We may even help others when we retell our stories, sharing lessons we've learned along the way.

Jesus's life is known to us today through stories about his life being told again and again, including his resurrection after death. The disciples and others kept the truth and memory of Jesus alive, leading to written accounts we read in the Bible. Today, changed lives continue to show the reality of Jesus, and we're thankful for the stories we have about his life.

May we remember stories—our own, others', and those from Scripture—that help us along our journey of life. And may we have opportunities to share our stories with others so that experiences we've had in life can help others along their journey.

Reflect

What encouraging story from my life do I want to intentionally remember this week?

Read

Mark 4:33-34: *Jesus used many stories like these to teach them. He taught them all that they could understand. He always used stories to teach them. But when he and his followers were alone together, Jesus explained everything to them.*

Pray

To keep the stories of Jesus close to my heart.
For my mind to be full of positive memories.

29

New Hampshire

PEACE

Anymore, it's rare when we travel as a family of four. Sometimes, though, John or Tricia will be with us for a short trip.

In May 2010, traveling as a family of four, we stopped at the Saint-Gaudens National Historic Site in New Hampshire. This is the home and workshop of sculptor Augustus Saint-Gaudens (1848–1907), a famous Irish American sculptor whose monuments are still in prominent places today.

We drove up the long lane to the entrance gate and walked around the grounds. The porch of the house where this artist lived has distinctive Greek-style columns, and purple gladiolas and huge red poppies were in full bloom in front of it. A mountain stood in the distance.

Some of Saint-Gaudens's sculptures and artwork are here. In a small courtyard was a bright golden-winged figure—something like a golden angel—that reflected in a still pool. Inside what is called the "Little Studio"—a workshop where the artist created some of his sculptures—is a wall of windows that lets in natural light. It must have been a quiet, lovely place to create art.

We saw a bronze statue that stands six feet tall, called "Diana"—a goddess standing on one leg, pointing a bow and arrow to her left. Standing next to the statue, Tricia struck the same pose with an imaginary bow and arrow, and we snapped a picture. On our way back to the car, we walked between rows of white birch trees, concluding our time in this beautiful place.

It's wonderful to be in a peaceful place with family, as well as to have peace within the family. We know that many families don't live in peace, though. Maybe that's because of internal conflicts that divide them, or things out of their control like war or poverty.

It's worth taking time to reflect on what we can do to help foster peace in our families—to consider the importance of developing harmonious relationships among our loved ones and doing what we can to have more peace in our daily lives.

Reflect

What helpful attitudes can I develop within myself that can bring more peace in my family?
Am I a peaceful influence on those around me?

Read

Philippians 4:7: *And God's peace will keep your hearts and minds in Christ Jesus. The peace that God gives is so great that we cannot understand it.*

Pray

To strive to live peacefully with others.
To relay peaceful feelings to my family members.

Photo Collage Video

You can view a 3-minute video featuring photos Gene and Marsha took at some of the places you're reading about in this book. Just add your name and email here to receive it immediately:

https://johnchristopherframe.com/photo-collage

30

New Jersey

LOYALTY

On March 27, 2013, we were sworn in to George Washington's army. At least that's what the reenactment soldier told us before we repeated the words of the oath he spoke to us.

It was Marsha's birthday, and we were at the Old Barracks Museum in New Jersey, built in 1758. It's a stone building, but what stood out were the large wooden balconies and stairways, all painted red. This place housed both British and American soldiers at different times.

On our visit, many people were in 1776-period costumes, appearing as if they were part of the Continental Army fighting in the American Revolutionary War. We saw reenactment soldiers marching in formation and horses being fed. Some soldiers were firing guns, reenacting what it was like to practice for battle.

Women were cooking pots of stew over an open fire. Others were washing clothes on washboards and shaking out blankets. Those in the infirmary wore nurse uniforms and were ready to care for those needing medical treatment.

Of course, this was all a reenactment. We were seeing a glimpse of the loyalty the people had to the American Revolution and some of their daily life experiences.

Before our swearing in, the sergeant called the visitors to come over to him. He was wearing white pants and a triangular-shaped black hat. His jacket was dark-blue and red, and his shoes were dusty. His long rifle was in front of him, the wooden stock on the ground and the barrel pointed to the sky. He held it with both hands as he waited in the sun.

He explained that he would be swearing us in to the army as new recruits for a three-year period, then told us to gather in formation if we agreed to this commitment. Without hesitation, we obeyed and then repeated after him the oath of allegiance.

For those who said this oath for real years ago, it was a commitment of loyalty to their country and allegiance as a faithful soldier. As Christians, when Jesus calls us to follow him, we are loyal. We obey. We love others. We follow Christ, serving him faithfully and seeking to live the holy life he's called us to live.

Reflect

How do I demonstrate my loyalty to Christ?

Read

John 14:15: *"If you love me, you will do the things I command."*

Pray

To follow Christ in my heart, mind, and actions.

31

New Mexico

PRAYER

The Loretto Chapel in Santa Fe, New Mexico, looks like a small cathedral that's been transplanted from Paris. It's beautiful inside and out.

Inside is the Miraculous Staircase. It's a tall, wooden spiral staircase at the back of the sanctuary. It curls up to the choir loft of the chapel. The staircase is twenty feet tall and has two 360-degree turns.

The craftmanship of this twisting staircase was a *whoa* moment for us—and probably everyone who visits. There is no center pole for support. For safety, handrails were installed later, as was an iron bracket for support. Instead of nails or screws, wooden pegs were used to keep the staircase together.

There's an interesting story about the Miraculous Staircase. In the late 1800s, the Sisters of Loretto had this church built. But unfortunately, the architect died before it was completed. One thing that was missing was a staircase to the choir loft, located high above the floor of the sanctuary. There was no way to get up there. Building a regular staircase would take up too much space, so the Sisters prayed for nine days to St. Joseph about it, believing he would intercede on their behalf to God. Their prayers were answered, and the Miraculous Staircase was completed.

The staircase spirals up from the floor to the choir loft, and the legend is that a carpenter appeared with simple tools and then disappeared when the staircase was finished. Interestingly, the wood used for the staircase is not native to the region.

This chapel is now a private museum. It preserves this spiral wooden wonder and the story behind it—one that's rooted in the prayers of Sisters seeking an answer to a problem they couldn't solve themselves.

They prayed for help. That's something we can do today too. Whether in a worship service, walking in a park, or anywhere else, we can pray. We can ask God for help with our problems, big or small.

Whether our prayers are of repentance or praise, or something else, we can call on God. He hears our prayers.

Reflect

What answers to prayer can I remember today?

Read

Philippians 4:6: *Do not worry about anything. But pray and ask God for everything you need. And when you pray, always give thanks.*

Pray

For faith that God hears my prayers and understands my needs.

32

New York

DEVELOPING

Ever since the Detroit Tigers won the World Series in 1984, we've enjoyed baseball and following this team. 1984 was our first year living in Michigan, and over the years we attended several games in Tiger Stadium. John loved baseball and began collecting baseball cards.

When we went on vacation to Maine, we visited the National Baseball Hall of Fame and Museum in Cooperstown, New York. The museum was crowded, but we took our time seeing everything we wanted to see.

We took a picture of John standing by the display of the hats Nolan Ryan wore during his no-hitter games, and standing next to a wooden statue of Babe Ruth at bat. We enjoyed looking at the wall display of baseball cards, including players from our childhood like Mickey Mantle.

We especially wanted to see the section related to the Tigers. Uniforms and bats were on display, along with photos of manager Sparky Anderson and others who were part of the 1984 World Series team.

Baseball players take years to develop into professional athletes. They practice and develop their skills in catching, throwing, and batting. They work with coaches and accept suggestions for how to improve so they develop and can reach their goals.

As Christians, we can develop in our relationship with God. We do this by reading Scripture and seeking guidance from the Holy Spirit. We listen to godly pastors and leaders. And we pray and worship.

Let's work on letting God develop us so that we reach the goal of not just entering heaven someday, but also of living the way God wants us to live here on earth.

Reflect

Am I developing into the person God wants me to be?

Read

Romans 12:2: *Do not be shaped by this world. Instead be changed within by a new way of thinking. Then you will be able to decide what God wants for you. And you will be able to know what is good and pleasing to God and what is perfect.*

Pray

For God to develop me so I live the way he wants me to live here on earth.

33

North Carolina

GUIDANCE

Over the years, Gene has enjoyed exploring his family roots, including searching for the graves of some of his distant relatives.

Gene's great-great-great-great-great-grandfather was Captain John Cox, a man who had served in the American Revolutionary War and owned about eight thousand acres of land in North Carolina. Gene had enough clues about where John Cox was buried that he thought he could find his grave, although he knew it would be a challenge. The grave isn't in a manicured cemetery but on the land he used to own.

The grave would have been impossible to find without some guidance along the way. We drove to the area where John Cox lived in North Carolina. It was a clear, sunny day in October. Amid the trees that were turning yellow, we saw road signs that told us we were in the correct vicinity.

On an adventure like this, the best people to seek guidance from are those who have lived in the area for a long time, so we stopped at a general store, where we met an elderly man who knew about the grave and also knew the current owner of the land. Following the man's directions, we found the owner's house, and Gene knocked on the door. A woman answered and said her husband was near the area of the property where the grave is.

To get there, we drove on a dirt lane with deep ruts that cut through a hilly Christmas tree farm. After less than a mile, afraid to go any farther, Gene got out of the car and walked toward a barn to meet the owner. The man told Gene where to find the grave, and Gene walked through a field of knee-high weeds and climbed a small fence to get there.

And there he found it—a four-sided gray monument in the middle of tall weeds. One side had John Cox's name and the date he died on it. Another side had his wife's name, though the dates of her birth and death were unknown, it said. The monument also had a couple of sentences about John Cox's life engraved on it. It was probably placed there years after he died.

Finding this grave was a wonderful adventure, and we know Gene couldn't have found it without the guidance he received along the way.

Life is full of journeys of one type or another. And they're not always smooth or easy to navigate. Thankfully, we can seek guidance to assist us through our challenges. Guidance can help us in ways we can't help ourselves. Of course, we need to be open to receiving guidance to benefit from it.

Reflect

> Whom do I seek guidance from when I experience a challenge?

Read

> Psalm 25:4-5: *Lord, tell me your ways. Show me how to live. Guide me in your truth. Teach me, my God, my Savior. I trust you all day long.*

Pray

For a quiet and pure heart to receive guidance from
the Holy Spirit.

Humility to know when I need guidance.

34

North Dakota

HELPING

Years ago, we watched the PBS documentary by Ken Burns about the Lewis and Clark Expedition.

In the early 1800s, Meriwether Lewis and William Clark explored portions of the West all the way to the Pacific Ocean. To carry out their task, they needed help from others. They took a group with them and received assistance from Native Americans who helped guide them.

Along the way, a man was hired as an interpreter for the exploration. He was married to a Native American woman named Sacagawea. She, along with their two-month-old baby, also joined the long journey, serving as an interpreter, as she spoke a language no one else in the group could speak.

To this day, Sacagawea is remembered for the help she provided on this exploration. She and her baby are featured on the front of the $1 Sacagawea coin, golden in color, and first minted in the year 2000.

In 2017, we took a train west, rented a car, and visited some sites in North Dakota that are related to the Lewis and Clark Expedition. We visited a replica of Fort Mandan—a camp that Lewis and Clark had built to stay one winter. Between the two wooden buildings was a flagpole with an American flag that had fifteen stars and fifteen stripes. It was at Fort Mandan that Lewis and Clark met Sacagawea and her husband.

Being an admirer of Sacagawea through the years, we've enjoyed learning about her and her family's role in the Lewis and Clark Expedition. Not only did Sacagawea and her husband help the group by interpreting across languages, but the presence of a Native woman and her baby let everyone they met know they were coming in peace.

Most of us today can't provide the kind of help to others that will be recorded in history books. But all of us can provide help to others in one way or another.

Maybe that's by saying a kind word to someone, helping a neighbor with a task, praying, or giving financial support.

As we live our lives, may we be inspired to help people in some small or big way.

Reflect

What is one way I can help someone today?

Read

Luke 6:31: *"Do for other people what you want them to do for you."*

Pray

To see opportunities to help others.

To allow others to help me when I need it.

35

Ohio

HOME

Ohio is our home. It's where we were born and raised. But we lived away from Ohio for many years.

Not too long after we got married in 1968, we moved to Florida so Gene could study for the ministry. We remember driving south on I-75 with our one-year-old daughter Tricia. We'd just left behind all our family and friends—everything we'd ever known—to move to a place we'd never been. It felt like a venture of faith. We were being obedient, even if that meant leaving behind our jobs and the brick home we just had built.

On our first day in Florida, after a normal afternoon rain shower, a beautiful rainbow appeared in the sky. To us, it was a sense of relief—a message from God saying "It will all be well."

Throughout our life together, we've had experiences we never dreamed of having. Through it all, our faith in God, prayer, and the prayers of others sustained us through life's difficulties.

We made many trips back to Ohio from our homes in Florida, Virginia, and Michigan. The sights along the highway became familiar landmarks. Driving on I-75, we'd pass the white dome of the Neil Armstrong Air & Space Museum in Wapakoneta, Ohio, that appears to be emerging from a grassy mound. And heading north on I-75 from Kentucky, we loved seeing the beautiful skyline of Cincinnati. At night, the buildings are lit up. Then we'd cross the Ohio River, pass the state line, and feel like we were home again.

When traveling back to Ohio, we had feelings of anticipation. We were excited to catch up with everyone. Later in life, we never knew if we might be seeing our parents, who were getting older, for the last time.

We returned permanently to Ohio in 2005 after thirty-three years away. The day we moved, another rainbow appeared in the sky. We saw it from our front porch. In our hearts, it reminded us of God's presence with us. We were where we should be—back home.

While Ohio was, and is now again, our home state, we await another home—our eternal one. Until then, we continue to trust God to be present with us here and wherever we go.

Reflect

How do I sense the presence of God when I am at home?

Read

Psalm 139:8-10: *If I go up to the skies, you are there. If I lie down where the dead are, you are there. If I rise with the sun in the east, and settle in the west beyond the sea, even there you would guide me. With your right hand you would hold me.*

Pray

To trust God to be present with me at home and wherever I go.

36

Oklahoma

BEAUTY FROM ASHES

On April 19, 1995, the Alfred P. Murrah Federal Building in Oklahoma City was bombed. In total, 168 people, including 19 children, were killed.

Where this building once stood is now a large outdoor memorial. This place—once buzzing with conversations among employees drinking coffee, the clicking of typewriters, and children playing in the daycare—is now hallowed ground. Where first responders met horrible chaos and lifeless bodies, is now quiet.

We visited this site twelve years after the bombing. The wreckage has now been transformed into a place where victims and survivors can be remembered in a peaceful ambiance.

Beauty from ashes.

There is a neatly manicured green lawn with 168 bronze-and-glass straight-backed chairs, each one memorializing a person who died in the bombing. Nineteen of the chairs are smaller, representing the children. The chairs are displayed in nine rows, symbolizing the nine stories of the building, and each chair is engraved with the name of someone who died on that floor. It's called the "Field of Empty Chairs," and next to it is a long, shallow reflecting pool.

Beauty from ashes.

On a chain link fence hangs pictures, key chains, beaded necklaces, and stuffed animals placed by visitors.

Beauty from ashes.

On what is called the Survivor Wall, more than six hundred names of people who survived are engraved in granite that was salvaged from the building.

Beauty from ashes.

A large American elm tree that survived the bombing is honored as the Survivor Tree. It continues to grow and flourish to this day.

Beauty from ashes.

To survive tragedies in life—big or small—we find ways of coping and mourning. Understandably, the "ashes" of what we've experienced or lost may cause despair. But through healing and time, we can hopefully experience peace again, feel joy instead of sadness, and see beauty from ashes.

Reflect

How can I help bring beauty to someone going through a challenging time?

Read

Revelation 21:1a, 3a, 4a: *Then I saw a new heaven and a new earth...I heard a loud voice from the throne. The voice said, "Now God's home is with men...He will wipe away every tear from their eyes. There will be no more death, sadness, crying, or pain..."*

Pray

For healing and transformation so I may experience beauty from ashes.

37

Oregon

PERSEVERANCE

Driving south from Washington to Oregon, Mount Hood—a snow-covered mountain—was on our left. It's the highest point in the state of Oregon and is a volcano, though it hasn't erupted for a long time.

This majestic mountain played an important role for people on the Oregon Trail—a popular route people followed as they went west to find a place to settle in the 1800s. They could see the mountain from far away, and it gave them inspiration and direction as they persevered in their travels west.

The Oregon Trail went from Missouri to Oregon City, Oregon, and was about two thousand miles long. About four hundred thousand people traveled it during the 1800s, with horses and oxen pulling covered wagons full of supplies. It was a journey of perseverance.

When we were in Idaho on an earlier trip, we saw ruts in the ground from wagon wheels on the Oregon Trail. That inspired us even more to see the end of the trail, in Oregon City. Upon arriving there, we visited the End of the Oregon Trail Visitor & Interpretive Center and learned about hardships people endured during their journey west. They were susceptible to diseases like cholera and typhoid. And they faced other adversities like snakebites and broken bones. Yet, their perseverance—and the hope that must have sustained them—brought them through the challenges they faced along the way.

As we all know, hardships didn't just come to those who lived a long time ago. We have them today too, in many different forms. And like the courageous early American settlers persevering through difficulties to travel west, may we find strength and hope as we experience our own challenges. May we keep our eyes on God through it all.

Reflect

How well am I keeping my eyes on God through the challenges I'm going through?

Read

2 Corinthian 4:16-18: *So we do not give up. Our physical body is becoming older and weaker, but our spirit inside us is made new every day. We have small troubles for a while now, but they are helping us gain an eternal glory. That glory is much greater than the troubles. So we set our eyes not on what we see but on what we cannot see. What we see will last only a short time. But what we cannot see will last forever.*

Pray

For strength through life's journey.

For wisdom and discernment to know when it may be best not to persevere on a certain path.

38

Pennsylvania

Brotherly Love

We visited Philadelphia, the largest city in Pennsylvania, on our wedding anniversary in March 2013. It was a beautiful sunny day.

The name "Philadelphia" combines the Greek words for beloved (*philos*) and brother (*adelphos*). So it's the "City of Brotherly Love."

We walked through Independence Hall, where the Declaration of Independence was signed in 1776. One can envision where Benjamin Franklin, Thomas Jefferson, and other founding fathers of America spoke with each other about the document. A short distance away is the home of the woman credited with making the first American flag, Betsy Ross. Marsha had hung the American flag on her porch as a child thousands of times, so seeing the large flags on display at Betsy Ross's home was thrilling for her.

We saw the Liberty Bell next. It's viewable through large windows 24 hours a day, 365 days a year. There is a large crack in the bell, and inscribed at its top is Leviticus 25:10b: "Proclaim liberty throughout all the land unto all the inhabitants thereof." Among other times, the Liberty Bell was rung on July 8, 1776, the day the Declaration of Independence was read publicly in Philadelphia.

We then made our way to find something else this city is known for—a Philly cheesesteak sandwich. There's no shortage of places to get one. We went to Sonny's Famous Steaks, where the thinly sliced ribeye steak, caramelized onions, and provolone cheese on a warm hoagie bun was delicious. It was an enjoyable day in Philadelphia, walking around and seeing important sites we'd heard about our whole lives.

Philadelphia—the City of Brotherly Love—was founded on the ideal of people living together peacefully. The Bible tells us, "Be kindly affectioned one to another with brotherly love" (Romans 12:10a KJV).

May we embody the brotherly love that allows us to live in friendship and peace with others. And may we keep this kind of love in our hearts every day.

Reflect

How can I better embody brotherly love and live more peacefully with others?

Read

Romans 12:9-10: *Your love must be real. Hate what is evil. Hold on to what is good. Love each other like brothers and sisters. Give your brothers and sisters more honor than you want for yourselves.*

Pray

To find ways to show love to others.

39

Rhode Island

HOPE

The state flag of Rhode Island is white with a gold anchor in the middle and gold stars in a circle around it. There is one word on the flag—"HOPE"—likely inspired by these words from the Bible: "hope we have as an anchor of the soul" (Hebrews 6:19a KJV).

As a small child, Marsha lived with her family in Rhode Island for a short time. Her father was stationed there in the U.S. Navy Reserves. This was during the Korean War, and people hoped and prayed for it to quickly end.

On a visit forty years later, we found the state to be beautiful. There are lovely towns, and mansions are built next to the ocean. Of course, many things have changed in this state over the years. We drove by the old Navy hospital—now closed—where one of Marsha's brothers was born in 1951. We also drove by the apartment building where Marsha's family lived, as well as a park where her mom would take her to play. The park looked smaller than it did in old pictures. In the early 1950s, there wasn't as much concrete or traffic, or as many buildings in the area. And while an old statue of a Navy hero is still there, the park now has a different name.

Over time, things change. That's the way life is. As the old saying goes, the only constant is change. So, it's important for us to keep hope in what we know will not change: God's love for us, salvation, heaven, the presence of the Holy Spirit, and so many other truths.

Whatever changes we may experience in life, we can try to keep hope in what is most important. Just like the Rhode Island state flag and the verse in Hebrews reminds us: May hope be our anchor.

Reflect

What can I think about that brings me hope?

How can I help others have more hope?

Read

Romans 15:13: *I pray that the God who gives hope will fill you with much joy and peace while you trust in him. Then your hope will overflow by the power of the Holy Spirit.*

Pray

To maintain hope.

For those who have little hope.

40

South Carolina

FRIENDS

In 2006, we were invited to join three other couples for a vacation in Hilton Head, South Carolina. One couple was related to us, and we'd known one of the others for many years. We've always traveled on our own or with our children, so this was a different kind of vacation experience.

We drove separately from the others, and on the way we visited relatives, saw the South Carolina State Capitol building, and went to a national park. We were surprised when we saw the other couples we'd be vacationing with inside the national park's visitor center. It was like they had come to surprise us. We all took a walk on the boardwalk trail at the park and then drove to Hilton Head. It was a wonderful way to begin our time together.

During this trip, not only did we see a lot of sites around Hilton Head, but we were also able to share these experiences with friends. We all walked on the huge *USS Yorktown* aircraft carrier, an 872-foot ship built during World War II. And we took a boat to Fort Sumter, the war fort where the American Civil War officially began in 1861.

One evening, we all went to a restaurant next to the harbor. After we ate, we climbed 114 steps to the top of the small red-and-white-striped lighthouse next to the restaurant. It had American flags flying in the wind at the top, and we looked out at the harbor, with white yachts and a long wooden boardwalk.

Back down near the beach, we watched the sun set over the harbor, shining its tangerine-orange light on the surface of the water. A thick blanket of clouds covered much of the sky, stretching out from the shore. But it stopped in a perfectly straight line, allowing us to see the glowing sun and a red-orange sky in the distance.

It was a memorable trip. We were able to deepen friendships with two couples we'd known for years and make a new friendship with the other couple. While the two of us are happy to travel on our own, it was refreshing to see sights with friends. We had conversations we wouldn't otherwise have had. The dynamics were completely different than if it had just been the two of us.

May we remember the importance of good friends—old ones and new ones. And if we're in need of more friends, may we do our best to invite others into our lives. Their lives and ours can be better because of it.

Reflect

What good memories do I have of spending time with friends?

Read

Proverbs 17:17a: *A friend loves you all the time.*

Pray

To be thankful for friends.

41

South Dakota

DISCOVERING

Not far from Mount Rushmore is a town called Custer, South Dakota. It's in the heart of the Black Hills, a mountain range in the northern part of the United States.

We were on a trip to see some of the West, including Yellowstone National Park, which you can read about later in this book. It was 1991—years before people learned about places on the internet prior to going on vacation. While driving in Custer, we discovered a family-owned shop—Ken's Minerals and Trading Post—that sold beautiful gems and handmade jewelry.

While visiting the shop, we learned they offered an opportunity to pan for gold. John was twelve years old, and this unique experience seemed like a fun activity. We couldn't pass it up.

We paid the fee, and a little while later the three of us were sitting with our feet in a shallow, cool creek in the middle of a field of three-foot-tall grass. Ken Spring, an eighty-two-year-old gold prospector and the owner of the shop, sat with us. He wore a cowboy hat with feathers on the front. His speech was slow, but he was a good storyteller.

Ken had shoveled dirt into large pans from a dirt pile next to the creek, and as we sat together, he showed us how to swirl the water in our pans, washing away dirt and removing larger stones, until the pans were nearly empty. We then would look for bright gold flakes and tiny agate gemstones in the remaining dirt in our pans.

It was a warm summer day, and we sat in the open sun, following Ken's instructions and listening to the stories he told about the history of the land. We were patient while we swirled around the dirt and water to see whether there was any gold to discover. Pretty soon, shiny flakes of gold, along with dark agates, appeared.

Being in nature with our feet in the water, we learned how to pan for gold and learned even more from the stories Ken shared with us. We felt the thrill of discovering gold, which had been hidden in the dirt unseen. We left with a small tube of the gold flakes and agates we'd found, which is still packed away in a drawer.

In life, sometimes we discover things we weren't expecting. Other times, we may discover something that was there all along that we just hadn't seen. And like the dirt in our pans that covered the gold flakes and agates, may our prayer be that God helps us discover things in our lives that may be covering over the bright, beautiful spirit he wants to shine through us.

May we fully discover the joy that comes with living close to God.

Reflect

What should I do, or not do any longer, to fully discover the joy that comes with living close to God?

Read

John 15:10-12: *"I have obeyed my Father's commands, and I remain in his love. In the same way, if you obey my commands, you will remain in my love. I have told you these things so that you can have the same joy I have. I want your joy to be the fullest joy.*

This is my command: Love each other as I have loved you."

Pray

To identify anything in my life that is hindering God's Spirit from shining through me.

42

Tennessee

GOD AND "GODS"

Tennessee is known for many things, such as
Nashville, Graceland, and the Great Smoky
Mountains National Park. But most aren't aware that
an exact replica of the Greek Parthenon is also in Tennessee. Located in Centennial Park, in Nashville, this
large structure was originally built in 1897. It was
rebuilt with concrete twenty-five years later, and still
stands tall and strong today.

The original Parthenon in Athens, Greece, was
a temple dedicated to the goddess Athena. It is
very old—built over four hundred years before Jesus was born—and is visited by millions each year.

The Parthenon in Nashville was carefully designed as a replica. It's about two-thirds the length of a football field and sixty-five feet tall. It has forty-six huge columns.

We visited the Nashville Parthenon on a bright, cold day in late December 2009. Beforehand, we had toured the Tennessee State Capitol and saw the grave of James Polk, the 11th president of the United States, who is buried next to the capitol.

Arriving at the Parthenon, we looked up at the stone carvings at the top, which are also replicas of the originals. They depict stories of Athena and Greek mythology.

Each god in Greek mythology has a story, like how Athena was born from the head of Zeus. Most people today probably don't believe these stories. We're not tempted to worship gods like Athena or Zeus. Yet, there are other "gods" that draw people to them—the hunger for possessions, money, power, and so on. Whatever might have a hold on us is something like a god, controlling us in some way or leading us away from holiness.

With God's help and healing, the Holy Spirit, and the power of Christ in us, we can live free of what draws us away from God's full sovereignty over our lives.

Reflect

What may have a hold on me?

Do I feel that the power of Christ in me is stronger than earthly things that draw me to them?

Read

1 Corinthians 8:6: *But for us there is only one God. He is our Father. All things came from him, and we live for him. And there is only one Lord—Jesus Christ. All things were made through Jesus, and we also have life through him.*

Pray

To be free of what draws me away from God's full sovereignty over my life.

43

Texas

MEMORIES

As we wrote in the devotion for California earlier in this book, our church's youth group went to San Diego for a youth convention in 1966. Traveling from Ohio across the country on two buses, we played games with our friends, relaxed, and watched the scenery.

On that journey, we drove through Texas, where there were prickly pear cacti and tumbleweeds rolling across the dry land. It was as if we were looking out at miles and miles of nothing. Despite this barren landscape, we were excited to see Texas and get closer to

California, our final destination. We had fun making new memories.

As we drove on Route 66, all of us on the bus sang "Get your Kicks on Route 66." The bus arrived in Amarillo, Texas, a real cowboy type of town, and we mailed postcards home. Marsha bought a charm shaped in the outline of Texas for a new bracelet she'd bought just for this trip. This was the first charm of many, and she still cherishes that bracelet with all those charms and the memories they represent.

We were all excited to cross the U.S.–Mexico border from El Paso, Texas, to Ciudad Juarez, Mexico. It was the first foreign country many of us would visit, and we were all thrilled. Ciudad Juarez was festive with gift shops and food vendors. Young boys outside were trying to get attention—holding up signs, being silly and high-spirited. We chatted with them and walked around to look for souvenirs. After several hours, we headed back across the border, returning to Texas and continuing our trip to San Diego. We still had a long way to go, which meant more hours on the bus and new opportunities to make memories.

As we reflect on the past and the memories we hold dear, let's ask God to help our minds be filled with more memories that bring us encouragement. Maybe these are memories of a long hug with someone we love, a beautiful sunset, or times we felt God's presence especially near us.

May these good memories of the past help us in our living today.

Reflect

What special, happy memory from my life can I remember throughout the rest of today?

Read

Psalms 143:5-6: *I remember what happened long ago. I recall everything you have done. I think about all you have made. I lift my hands to you in prayer. As a dry land needs rain, I thirst for you.*

Pray

To remember experiences from my life that encourage me.

To live in a way that, through my daily interactions, I help bring about positive memories to those around me.

44

Utah

SALT

It was sunny and hot during our visit to Utah in 2008. Driving west on I-80, we noticed what looked like snow stretching for miles. But it was July and this wasn't snow. It was salt. The sun was reflecting off the Great Salt Lake Desert. It was so bright it was almost blinding.

We'd also just driven near the famous Great Salt Lake. It's very large but is slowly drying up, getting smaller as the water level lowers over time. This has become a crisis. A university report urged water conservation, predicting that the lake, as it's known today, will be dry by 2028 if loss of water because of water overuse in the region continues.[1]

Believe it or not, the Great Salt Lake is saltier than the ocean. We all know that salt enhances the flavor of food, but it has other uses too. It's used to preserve meat and melt ice. And you can gargle with salt water when your throat hurts.

In what is referred to as the Sermon on the Mount, Jesus told his disciples, "You are the salt of the earth" (Matthew 5:13a). By being the salt of the earth, we live out the Gospel for others. And that passion shouldn't dry up. We need more of that.

When love is in our hearts, it can be the salt that melts hate and brings healing to the brokenhearted. Let us seek to live as the "salt of the earth" that Jesus calls us to be.

Reflect

In what ways can I better live out the Gospel for others?

Read

> Matthew 5:13-16: *"You are the salt of the earth. But if the salt loses its salty taste, it cannot be made salty again. It is good for nothing. It must be thrown out for people to walk on.*
>
> *You are the light that gives light to the world. A city that is built on a hill cannot be hidden. And people don't hide a light under a bowl. They put the light on a lampstand. Then the light shines for all the people in the house. In the same way, you should be a light for other people. Live so that they will see the good things you do. Live so that they will praise your Father in heaven."*

Pray

> That I live out Jesus's words to be the salt of the earth and light for other people.

---

1. B. W. Abbott et al., "Emergency measures needed to rescue Great Salt Lake from ongoing collapse," January 4, 2023, https://doi.org/10.131 40/RG.2.2.22103.96166.

45

Vermont

STRENGTH

On our New England vacation when we stopped at the Baseball Hall of Fame and went to Maine, which we wrote about earlier, we saw several covered bridges in Vermont.

There are about one hundred covered bridges in this state. Covered bridges are strong and durable, and last for many years. Made of wood, they have a roof to protect them from rain and snow, and usually have walls. They serve an important purpose, bridging two sides of rivers and creeks. They are also beautiful and nostalgic.

In Vermont, we took pictures of the covered bridges we visited. For years, these photos hung on the wall of Gene's office at the church.

Driving from New Hampshire to Vermont, we crossed the Cornish-Windsor Bridge that connects these two states. This covered bridge is 449 feet long and is one of the longest covered bridges in the United States. It was built over the Connecticut River in 1866 and is still in use today. On the New Hampshire side of the bridge there is a sign above the entrance that reads "WALK YOUR HORSES OR PAY TWO DOLLARS FINE." The bridge is painted white and has open-air windows letting in light and air. Most, if not all, of the bridge is technically in the state of New Hampshire.

After driving across it and entering Vermont, one of the other bridges we visited was the Hammond Covered Bridge. It has a surprising history. It was built in 1842 over Otter Creek and is 139 feet long. During the large flood of 1927, this bridge floated more than a mile downstream and settled in a field. Imagine that—a bridge being lifted up in a flood and carried downstream more than a mile. Remarkably, it stayed intact and was put back in its original location.

Like the Hammond Covered Bridge that didn't break apart when it was washed away in flood waters, when we experience rain and floods in our own lives, literally or figuratively, we also want to stay strong.

During life, we may experience great suffering. We may feel "washed away" by the flood of burdens. But in Christ, not only can we find strength to get through the difficult days, but we can also find hope. Through strength in Christ, we can endure life's difficulties and trust him to lead us through the storm.

Reflect

When have I found strength in Christ to get through difficulties?

Read

Ephesians 6:10: *Finally, be strong in the Lord and in his great power.*

Pray

For strength and hope during the rains and floods of life.

46

Virginia

ENCHANTING

Virginia was our home for eight years when Gene pastored the Community Church of God in Arlington. We had many opportunities to visit parks and historical places, and this was where John was born.

In early November 2016, long after we moved away from the state, we drove along the Blue Ridge Parkway to see fall colors. The Blue Ridge Parkway is a long, scenic road designed for travelers to see beautiful views of the Blue Ridge Mountains. The northern half of the parkway is in Virginia and the southern half is in

North Carolina, and the road is full of enchanting places to experience the majesty of God's creation.

The weather was crisp and clear, and traffic was heavy. As we drove from North Carolina to Virginia on the parkway, we saw a deer near the road that was eating among fallen, dried leaves. We visited the Mabry Mill in Virginia, built in 1910. Made of wood that is now grayed and weathered over time, it's a historical building whose picture belongs on a wall calendar. A sign said it was the most photographed feature on the parkway.

When it was built, the Mabry Mill grounded corn into corn meal, and a wood saw was also powered by the mill. You can hear water flowing through wooden troughs as it flows to the top of the mill's large water wheel. It then pours onto the water wheel, making it spin. The water then spills into a small pond. Like a mirror, the mill is reflected on the pond's calm surface, making the site even more enchanting.

Later, we stopped and walked on the Appalachian Trail. We've always enjoyed learning about this hiking trail, which passes through fourteen states. While driving the Blue Ridge Parkway, we were excited to see signs marking where it crossed the road.

In various places over the years, we've walked on some of the Appalachian Trail for a brief amount of time. So, this day, we walked on the trail for about fifteen minutes. Most of the leaves had fallen from the trees, and the forest was looking more like winter. We quickly realized the trail was a little too difficult for us. After taking a couple of pictures, we got back in the car and continued our journey.

Being in the mountains and experiencing the enchantment and wonder they hold can remind us to be thankful—for nature and the opportunity to be in places that quiet our minds.

In a couple of days, we'll share about the ending of this trip through the mountains after we left Virginia and went to West Virginia. And in our next devotion, on the state of Washington, we'll share about seeing the beauty of God's creation.

Reflect

How can feelings about special experiences I've had help me remember the presence of God?

Read

Psalm 90:2: *Before the mountains were born, and before you created the earth and the world, you are God. You have always been, and you will always be.*

Pray

To thank God for special times and opportunities.

Want to see some of the places in this book?

You can watch a 3-minute photo collage video featuring some pictures from Gene and Marsha's travels. Just add your name and email here: https://johnchristopherframe.com/photo-collage

---

47

Washington

CREATION

At Olympic National Park, we had a picnic at a place 5,200 feet high in elevation, with a beautiful panoramic view. It was sunny, and we marveled at the snow-capped mountains in the distance.

We chose a picnic table near the parking lot and had deli sandwiches, chips, and soft drinks we'd bought at a grocery store earlier that day. These had been kept cool in the plastic cooler we brought from home in one of our suitcases. We've always loved having picnics, and this spot in the mountains was one of the most beautiful picnic areas we'd ever been to. It was the perfect place to enjoy God's creation.

After our picnic, we visited a ninety-foot-tall waterfall in the park, Marymere Falls. At the top, water flows straight down, cascading over rocks so that the width of the waterfall increases as the water falls down into the stream below.

To get there, we walked on an easy trail through a forest with tall spruce trees and dark-green vines. We crossed a narrow log bridge on the trail—Marsha keeping both hands on the railing to stay safe. At the waterfall, we felt cool mist in the air and saw children splashing water at each other, squealing, and having fun.

It may be surprising, but there are rain forests in Olympic National Park. It rains there often in the winter. Giant trees and hanging moss create a canopy of green, and heavy dew drips down from above. We hadn't seen anything like this before. There are ferns and large fallen trees on the ground, and we saw Roosevelt elk with their calm and playful calves.

In one of the rain forests is a tree thought to be about one thousand years old. It's the Quinault Big Sitka Spruce tree, and it's 191 feet tall. We had our picture taken standing in front of it.

Thinking back on this trip, the beautiful scenery, and all we experienced being in God's creation, the song "How Great Thou Art" comes to mind. We felt awesome wonder when seeing the greatness God had created.

Reflect

When was a time I saw or felt the majesty of God in creation?

How can I be more intentionally aware of God's creation around me?

Read

Psalm 95:3a, 4-6: *The Lord is the great God. ...The deepest places on earth are his. And the highest mountains belong to him. The sea is his because he made it. He created the land with his own hands. Come, let's bow down and worship him. Let's kneel before the Lord who made us.*

Pray

To live in a way that honors God's creation, remembering it is his.

48

West Virginia

CROSSING OVER

After visiting the Blue Ridge Parkway, which we wrote about in the Viriginia devotion, we drove across the Appalachian Mountains of West Virginia.

The red, orange, and yellow leaves of the oak and maple trees were mixed with the green of the pines and hemlocks. In one spot, we got out of the car and took a picture of steep, tree-covered mountains with the New River flowing through a valley between them.

We also drove across the New River Gorge Bridge. This isn't just any bridge. It's the third-highest bridge in the United States. It was chosen to be the symbol of West Virginia on the back of the U.S. quarter when the state commemorative quarters were minted.

This bridge crosses over the huge chasm of open space above the river. When it was completed in 1977, it shortened the journey from one mountain to the other—across the valley and river—by forty minutes. Now, the drive across the bridge is short. Families and friends can be easily united, and travelers can more easily get to where they need to go.

Bridges allow us to easily get from one side to the other. Each one spans a space that, without it, would be impossible or very difficult to cross over. Like a deep valley between large mountains, sin separates us from God. All kinds of attempts have been made to ease the pain of this separation. But these efforts fall short of God's eternal plan to bring us back into right relationship with him.

In Jesus, God himself came to earth. In following Jesus and living the way He's called us to live, we have the "bridge" over sin and despair, allowing us to cross over and receive the blessing of living in right relationship with God and gaining eternal life.

In crossing over the chasm between us and God, we believe in Christ's resurrection, recognize and repent of our sin, and live in obedience to him.

Reflect

Have I crossed over what separates me from God? Is anything preventing me from living in right relationship with God?

Read

Ephesians 2:13: *Yes, at one time you were far away from God. But now in Christ Jesus you are brought near to God through the blood of Christ's death.*

Pray

To live the way God has called me to live so that nothing separates me from him.

49

Wisconsin

DECISIONS

When John was a child, we took a car trip to Yellowstone National Park in Wyoming. Tomorrow, in our devotion on Wyoming, we share something about our time in that state.

From our home in Michigan, we made stops along the way as we drove across the country. The first place we visited on this trip was Wisconsin Dells, Wisconsin. Walking around the town, we visited the little shops there and bought fudge. We stayed a couple of nights in a rustic cabin at a KOA campground, and Gene cooked dinner on the grill.

We bought tickets for a guided boat tour on the Wisconsin River. The river was pea-green, and from the boat we were able to see the natural sandstone cliffs and scenic rock formations this area is known for. One of the spots we passed was Chimney Rock—a geological formation with layers of sandstone shaped like a chimney.

At some point along the journey, we all got off the boat to explore the area. As a group, we gathered to watch the famous "dog leap," where a large trained dog jumped a short distance from the edge of a cliff to a flat-topped natural rock tower fifty feet above us. Then it jumped back to its owner and got a treat. We all applauded.

That dog, and other trained dogs like it, have performed this "dog leap" show countless times, jumping from the edge of the cliff to the flat-topped rock tower and then back. Every time, as it runs and anticipates what it needs to do, the dog must discern and decide when to make the actual jump—not too soon and not too late. Then, returning to its owner, the dog discerns and decides when and how to safely make the leap again. These days, there is a net below just in case the dog falls.

In our lives, we make decisions every day. Some are small, some are big. While some decisions are more important than others, they all affect us—and others around us—in one way or another.

May we seek God's wisdom and feel God's Spirit giving us direction as we discern and make decisions, big and small.

Reflect

What decision am I currently thinking about?
Am I seeking God's wisdom about it?

Read

Psalm 25:4-5: *Lord, tell me your ways. Show me how to live. Guide me in your truth. Teach me, my God, my Savior. I trust you all day long.*

Pray

To live so I can feel God's Spirit as I make decisions each day.
For God's help in making decisions.

50

Wyoming

RENEWAL

After we left Wisconsin Dells, which we wrote about in yesterday's devotion, we continued our journey west, eventually making it to Yellowstone National Park in Wyoming. We stayed four nights at Old Faithful Inn, inside the park. The bathroom was down the hall rather than inside the room.

In front of the inn is the most famous geyser in the park, called Old Faithful. It shoots boiling water up over one hundred feet in the air about every hour or hour and a half. Crowds gather around to watch it, and as it erupts, steam from the hot water blows in the wind.

Something else that's interesting in the park is the hot, bubbling mud pools that look like thick gray paint. Bubbles pop on their surface, with each bubble different than another. Hydrogen sulfide gas comes up through the mud, and you can smell a strong, disturbing odor—like rotten eggs.

One of our best memories of that trip is the Chuck Wagon Cookout we enjoyed one evening in the park. We rode in a covered wagon to get to the cookout, while John rode a horse for two hours, meeting us there for dinner.

Walking on trails in the park, we saw devastation from the largest forest fire in Yellowstone National Park's history. It happened in 1988, three years before our visit. Nearly 800,000 acres—36 percent of the park—burned. We saw dead trees that had burned in the fire, and in the worst areas, the ground was still gray or light brown and bare. It gave us an eerie feeling, knowing that the area had been engulfed in flames. Further destruction had resulted from the mountain pine beetle, which had killed many whitebark pine trees. Also, it hadn't rained in a long time the year we visited.

Yet, despite all that, we saw new plants growing. The forest was rejuvenating. Minerals from the ash, sunlight, and rain allowed plant life to grow. Amid all the destruction around us, life was returning. There was renewal in the forest.

And just like in the forest, renewal can come to us even when we've been harmed or feel burned out from stress and difficulties. Christ's love can renew our hearts and lives after we've experienced pain. We can be resurrected from spiritual death. Joy can replace fatigue. Peace can follow stress.

Through renewal in Christ, our lives can be changed, and with that, those around us too.

Reflect

Where in my life do I need renewal?

Read

Ephesians 4:23-24: *But you were taught to be made new in your hearts. You were taught to become a new person. That new person is made to be like God—made to be truly good and holy.*

Pray

For love to renew my life.

To be the renewed person God wants me to be so I can positively impact those around me.

Conclusion

BY JOHN CHRISTOPHER FRAME

We hope the devotions in this book have inspired and strengthened you in your spiritual journey.

As for my parents, they're getting older but still travel when they can. My parents have lived simple lives, and the traveling they've done wasn't luxurious. In recent years, they drove to all eighty-eight county courthouses in Ohio, their home state. They took short trips to see a few at a time, snapping a picture of each one, and going inside the buildings when they could.

Mostly, though, their "travels" nowadays relate to going to my mom's doctor's appointments. Sometimes they make the experience fun by getting donuts and then driving to a local park to eat them after the appointment. It's a simple way to enjoy the journey they're on together, even to a doctor's appointment.

My parents purchased their cemetery plots a few years ago and now have a gravestone that marks their future final resting place. They had the gravestone engraved with a sketch of two people walking in nature, words from a Bible verse, and the phrase "Thanks for the journey."

My parents are grateful for the journey of life they've shared, and for God's presence with them. Through their nearly sixty years of marriage, they've supported each other and intentionally sought God to be at the center of their life together.

My parents' travels and the experiences they've had together have shaped their relationship. We hope the devotions in this book can help shape your spiritual development and relationship with God.

As you continue your own spiritual journey, may the themes of some of these devotions—like refreshment (Arkansas), praise (Maine), and hope (Rhode Island)—remind you to grow closer to God and those you love.

Quick Favor?

We hope you've enjoyed this book and that you'll tell others about it.

Can you rate the book and possibly write a review at the online store where you purchased or downloaded it?

Ratings and reviews are important for authors to help them get the word out about their books.

And they help future readers know whether a book is for them too.

Could you take a minute or two to leave an honest review? It can be as short as one sentence. You can also simply rate the book without writing anything.

It's a big help. Thank you!

Want to read one more devotion?

There's a devotion from Georgia that couldn't fit into this book. It takes you to President Jimmy Carter's hometown and invites you to reflect on legacy—how you hope to be remembered. Here is the link to receive it by email:

https://johnchristopherframe.kit.com/bonus -devotion

Stay connected!

Want more devotions and never-before-released content from John Christopher Frame?

Sign up to receive his updates here:

http://johnchristopherframe.com/stay-conne cted

Want more support on your spiritual journey?

Check out this free 7-day devotional.

7 Days to Upping Your Prayer Life, Loving Others, and Having More Joy by John Christopher Frame offers insightful guidance for Christians seeking to renew their quiet time with God through devotions and intentional reflection.

Download this free devotional now that readers describe as powerful, easy to read, and life-giving. Refocus on what truly matters and begin a transformative week-long journey. Grab it for free:

http://www.johnchristopherframe.com/prayer

About the Authors

H. Eugene Frame and his wife, Marsha, love traveling together, exploring the history and beauty of the places they visit. Gene has a longtime interest in family genealogy and enjoys listening to people's stories. In 2005, after living in three other states, he and Marsha moved back to Ohio, the place they call home. Gene began pastoring in 1975 and currently serves as a Bible teacher in the church he and Marsha attend.

Marsha Frame taught adult education and has served as a Sunday school teacher, sharing her love of learning and faith. Over the years, she has enjoyed reading, singing in church, daily devotions, walking in parks, and traveling. Marsha and her husband, Gene, have been married for nearly sixty years and have two grown children, Tricia and John.

John Christopher Frame is an author who helps readers deepen their spiritual journey. He has lived internationally for most of his adult life and has traveled to all sixteen towns in present-day Turkey mentioned in the Book of Acts that the Apostle Paul visited. John enjoys budget-friendly adventures, exploring outdoor markets, and going to cafés in his neighborhood. You can check out his free 7-day devotional and other books at http://www.johnchristopherframe.com.

Other Books by John Christopher Frame

Homeless at Harvard: Finding Faith and Friendship on the Streets of Harvard Square is an unforgettable story of John's summer with the community of people who were homeless near Harvard University. In this unique book, you'll meet John's companions on the streets as they share their own voices—challenging how we think about people experiencing homelessness.

7 Attitudes of the Helping Heart: How to Live Out Your Faith and Care for the Poor is an easy-to-read book designed to show you how to keep your faith central in all you do and help you move into the joy of loving others more. It includes first-person narratives that provide a window into the lives of people experiencing poverty.

7 Days to Upping Your Prayer Life, Loving Others, and Having More Joy is a 7-day devotional book that offers insightful guidance to help you renew your quiet time with God through devotions, prayer, and intentional reflection.

Increase Your Leadership Impact: 6 Simple Strategies to Connect with God's Wisdom, Make Tough Decisions, and Inspire Those Around You is a short, easy-to-read book that walks you through simple tips to help you feel closer to God and grow in your ability to lead those around you.

Visit John's website to learn more:
http://www.johnchristopherframe.com